DANNY PRINCE II

# It Had to Happen

When God Qualifies the Disqualified

# Praise for It Had to Happen

*It Had to Happen* is a powerful, passionate, and inspiring message reminding us that how we respond is more important than what happens to us. If you have ever felt disqualified or not enough, this book is for you!

Tayo Tychus, Pastor of Abundant Life Chapel

If you ever have found yourself imprisoned by the fear of failure or your confidence paralyzed by rejection after rejection, *It Had to Happen* is the book for you! Danny Prince II has always had an incredible way of telling a story but has finally took to translating his stories of rejection to triumph, pain to progress, loss to hope, into a book which was both inspiring and gives readers insight to how you can overcome any obstacle that comes your way. Danny has a story to tell and *It Had to Happen,* from start to finish, shows the passion in Danny's heart to help others, and it comes to life through each and every word written in this work of art. I am immensely proud of Danny's work.

Joseph D. Snider, CLC, LCSW-C, LICSW, Therapist, Author, and Friend

Danny!!! *It Had to Happen* is phenomenal!! OMG!! I am blown away, it touched my heart and hit home in so many areas. This book is going bless the masses!!! Your transparency and authenticity radiates through the pages!! Thank you for allowing me to be one of the first to read and to endorse this body of work. It has indeed been a pleasure reading, it blessed me immensely! I am beyond proud and love you so, so much!!

Connie Gilmore, Founder of Premature Widow; Speaker; Author; Motivator; Widow Advocate; Relationship Advocate.

*It Had to Happen: When God Qualifies the Disqualified* displays a relatable truth that exposes many of our issues around the topic of rejection. This book provides relevancy to the experience of not feeling qualified and being excluded in life, which all too often determines our potential and strips us of our true greatness. The transparency is refreshing and relative to many of our life journeys to becoming. This book will cause the reader to dig into their inner struggles while simultaneously providing healing and deliverance.

Dr. Shakina D. Rawlings, Pastor of Kingdom Fellowship Church, CEO of S.D. Rawlings Enterprise

*It Had to Happen* is a vulnerable read that compels tenacity and really reminds you of the purpose of faith. From start to finish, I felt seen AND loved by God. Great read for anyone looking to find the lemonade in what may feel like a life of lemons.

Linnita Hosten, Author, Speaker, and Owner of Excellence Brainery, LLC

Published by ELOHAI International Publishing & Media:
P.O. Box 1883
Cypress, Texas 77410
elohaipublishing.com

For inquiries or to request bulk copies, e-mail hello@elohaiintl.com.

For more information about the author or to book him for an event, please visit www.dannyprinceii.com

ISBN: 978-1-953535-29-0

# Table of Contents

# Dedication

To my Lord and Savior, Jesus Christ, thank you! Who I am, my very being, and everything I do is all because of you—who saved me, protected me, kept me, poured into me, and gave me everything I needed to speak life into this book. It is my desire that in all things I say and do, you would get all the glory.

To my amazing wife and best friend, Angela (My Angel), you are my rock, my peace, and my balance! Without you, I am so off-centered. You're a major inspiration to me, and I am motivated by your very presence. You helped me stay on track, you pushed and held me accountable to finish what I desired to accomplish. And for that, you will forever be my life partner in love, marriage, business, and in life.

To my three beautiful, anointed, and incredible daughters: Aaryn, Avery, and Allyson, please know that this is all because of you three and mommy. You all are the reason I pressed when I felt like giving up—the reason I worked as hard as I did when I felt like quitting, the reason I started writing again after years of being stagnant. And as I continue to try my hardest to build a legacy that you all can stand on and carry in years to come, you four are my greatest inspiration!

May this book serve as a tool and an additional road map on your journey in life so that when setbacks happen, because they will, you will not get run down, run over, or paralyzed by them. But you will know that they are there to serve as a catapult to your future. Every setback, rejection, failed attempts not approved, and disqualification you receive in life is the indicator that God is in control of the things you feel you have lost control over. Consider this book a baton that I hand to each of you to run on and live **your** dreams, pursue **your** goals, and tell **your** story!

To my Mom, Carolyn A. Jiggetts, thank you for being the example of never giving up. You are the reason I have the determination to keep going, the reason I have passion in everything I do. Mom, you raised me for such a time as this, to tell somebody that through all the hell we go through in life, **It Had to Happen** to get us to where we need to be. Your life is a prime example of just that! I love you Ma.

To my brother, Joseph D. Snider, thank you! You ignited the fire to bring my first book to fruition. You were a listening ear, and you gave me the initial tools, the plans, and the blueprint to make all this possible. I am very appreciative of you and hope that one day I will be as good of a writer and author as you. Thank you, Brother!

To Natasha T. Brown and your amazing ELOHAI International Publishing and Media Team, you were such a perfect and timely alley-oop to an amazing dunk in the finishing and publishing of my first book. From the time we connected and I was led to be a part of your 30-Day Book Writing Challenge, I knew God was getting ready to birth this book out of me, and you were the coach and midwife to make it happen. For that, I am so grateful for you and your team.

Last but not least, to the readers of this book—those who have suffered and dealt with more setbacks, rejections, disapprovals, failures, and disqualifications than you can count. May you find hope in the words in this book, to know that **God** is your Qualification even when you feel Disqualified—that is why you are **still standing!**

> **For I reckon that the suffering of this present time is not worthy to be compared to the glory which shall be revealed. (ROMANS 8:18)**

# Introduction

**You're fired! You've failed! You did not get approved! You don't qualify! You did not get accepted! You will not advance to the next grade! You did not get selected for the position! Your skill set does not meet the qualifications we're looking for! You've been disqualified! We went with another candidate, and your services are no longer needed here!**

Now that I have your attention. How did it make you feel to read those statements? They sounded pretty discouraging to hear, right? I thought so too. However, if I can be honest with you, throughout my life, I think I've heard just about every rejection phrase listed above on more than one occasion. And each time, I really wish I can tell you I shrugged my shoulders, brushed it off, and bounced back easily, boldly, and with more confidence than before. Unfortunately, that was not the case. My rejections took me to a very dark and isolated place where I had to maneuver through the deep and dark areas of my feelings and find my way back to the surface. I had to face what I wished I could have run away from forever.

In this book, I will share with you several personal life stories. I will share my hurts, my unsuccessful attempts, my failures, pushbacks, and rejections. And most importantly, in the midst of literally almost losing everything I had (including my sanity), I was constantly turned down, turned away, and rejected, yet somehow, God used every ounce of my failures and unsuccessful attempts to show me how **only he** can **restore the rejected, develop the displaced, lift the losers, and qualify the disqualified**! But before I get too excited, let me slow down and slow walk this journey. Let's start from the beginning, the very bottom, inside your pit, your lion's den, your fiery furnace, inside the belly of your whale, and the back of the line. Let's start right there!

Several times in my life, young and old, I heard and experienced one of the hurtful and discouraging statements above, if not all of them. Such negative comments and experiences can create an umbrella of internal storms that cause severe damage to one's physical, emotional, and mental confidence and self-esteem. It can also cause paralysis and any chance of bouncing back, moving forward, recovering, or simply getting up to try again.

An article in the American Psychological Association said, "As researchers have dug deeper into the roots of rejection, they've found surprising evidence that the pain of being excluded is not so different from the pain of physical injury." I know this statement to be true because after every moment of feeling excluded, rejected, and disqualified, a sense of physical pain came out of nowhere and lingered in my gut, as if I was punched and knocked down. It's a harsh comparison, yet it's the reality some face. I remember my mother used to say, "Life can be so cruel at times." And more often than less, I saw the very thing my mother would say come to light. Life can be very cruel.

The familiar phrase comes to mind, "Whenever I take three steps forward, life finds a way to knock me five steps back." The illusion is created as if life has only one mission, and that mission is to shoot down every ounce of potential happiness, success, achievement, and greatness. At any given time, while you're being kicked down, counted out, rejected, and displaced, life has the audacity to grab you by the hand. It escorts you down the red carpet to be seen on every platform and social media page to a front-row seat, with popcorn, nachos, and a Cherry Coke. And just like that, you're watching everyone else around you—succeeding and getting promoted, elevated, getting married, having babies, graduating, and achieving so much in life. Yes, this is the life we're living. Or is it?

Allow me to answer that for you. Yes, this **is** the life we're living. But no, we're not living in this permanent reality of what seems to be an eternity of forever setbacks, rejections, and failures. Repeat after me, "**This too shall pass!**" When you understand that, you can see the bright side of a cloudy day. Life is made up of several **wins** and many **failed** attempts. You will win some and lose some. In some cases, you win a little more, and at other times, you might lose even more. But it is very easy to stick your chest out and walk in your success, your victory, and your achievement when you're constantly winning. But how do you hold your head up, stick your chest out, and walk in that same success, victory, and achievement when you're constantly losing, or you've already lost so much. It is my prayer that this book will help you take every loss you encounter and find a way to learn from it, trust God in it, and turn whatever you're going through into a win. Or even in the midst of your loss, God will allow you to find your win!

My brothers and sisters, do not sit back and do not buckle your seatbelt. I highly encourage you not to keep your hands and feet inside the vehicle during this journey. Because what you're about to read and experience will make you want to lift your hands and move your feet. Through the power of God in this book, you're about to witness and experience how to be delivered from people's thoughts and perceptions. This includes your own thoughts, perception, and negative thinking about who you are and where you may be heading in life. So here you are now and life has thrown you more than enough lemons. **Now** it's time to make lemonade!

**It Had to Happen: When God Qualifies the Disqualified!**

## chapter 1

# Disqualified—What Do You Mean?

*Being disabled should not mean being disqualified from having access to every aspect of life.*

*—Emma Thompson*

What does it mean to be disqualified? What feelings, memories, or series of events does the word "disqualify" bring to you? What picture comes to mind when you think about the times you felt like you didn't qualify? As you read this book, it is my desire that every page, story, and illustration you read comes from a place of transparency. I want the words to be authentic and not another cut-and-paste book that lacks transparency. I will refer to the process of being disqualified as being **rejected, set back, counted out, left out, disapproved, failed,** and several other terms that could be used to eliminate you from life's possibilities. So do not get so caught up in the word "disqualify" that you miss the message. The message I want you to take away is that while you may have been disqualified, it is GOD who qualifies all things. He is the one who validates you when everyone else has counted you out!

## It Had to Happen

If you were to ask twenty people what it means to be disqualified, you would get twenty different answers, twenty different stories, and twenty different emotions to go with those actions. My stories and testimonies will not be yours. You may be able to relate, but you have your own story to tell. Yet one thing will be the same across the board—at some point, as you experience any of these moments, they can and will stop you dead in your tracks. They will leave you lost and confused, questioning if you could have done anything differently to enact a different outcome. But why did it happen? Someone could experience denials, obstacles, or being excluded for many reasons—in many different shapes and sizes.

But I'd like to entertain the question "**How does one get disqualified**"? I decided to categorize my answers. I have personally encountered at least twenty different ways. But to paint a vivid picture of what it means and what it looks like to be disqualified, I broke it down into three sections: *Life*, *People*, and *Inadequacies & Limitations*. I chose these sections because every single day, from the time you wake up to the time you go to sleep, you **have** to face these three. So unless you're dead, life will always be a factor. Unless you're locked away in solitary confinement, you will have to deal with people. And unless you're Jesus Christ himself, you will deal with some form of inadequacies & limitations. Any one of these will attempt to cause many delays and hindrances.

**Life**—Life has a way of presenting major obstacles and defeats. And as our elders would say, "If you've lived just a little while, life will bring you some trials!" I remember a critical time in my life in 2008. My wife and I had just gotten married in October and purchased our first home only a few months before the wedding. Several months after the wedding, we began having the conversation of adding to our family. At this time, my wife and I were making a collective salary of approximately one hundred thousand dollars, annually. I was working as a contractor for the Federal Government, and my wife was working for a private firm as an executive administrator.

When I tell you that life was great, it was the perfect setting for a romantic love story! We were just married, we were enjoying life in our new home, and we were making pretty decent money. Yet little did we know that eight months into our fairytale book story, life would present us with a huge test, in the form of a major setback that would rock our world! Ironically, my wife and I were both laid off from our respective jobs. We did not see this coming, and it most certainly was not the hand we wanted to be dealt. Naturally, our instinct was to go into full panic mode, pulling out our hair and stressing over this major setback that we were not ready for and had not planned for. We definitely didn't need this in that season of our lives.

Our backs were hard-pressed against the wall—we were having the conversation about bringing a baby into this world, we had a mortgage and utilities to pay, we were only eight months into our marriage trying to navigate through our honeymoon stage. This setback made me feel like I was losing before the race even got started. I felt like I had failed before the test was even administered, and I felt like I was being set up before I was even given a chance to succeed. This may not be your story, this may not be your testimony, but this is what being disqualified looked like to me and so many others. How would we bounce back; how would things turn around for me and my family? I was a man trying to build a family—with a new house, a car, and no job.

How would I cover, protect, and provide for my family? God, did I just get disqualified?

When you've been placed in a situation where you feel like you're losing everything, life really starts to get blurry. This season of my life was a very low, long, and drawn-out season. But God gave my wife and me the peace over the years to see that while we thought we were losing everything, God was gaining more of our attention. He showed us that he had control over even the material things we lost. It was God who kept us afloat to provide us both with jobs, to bless us to birth our first daughter, and to remain in that house for over ten years. We thought we were losing something during that time, but we actually gained more. We stopped worrying and began trusting. We stopped counting ourselves out and started counting on God even more. We saw God bring Scripture to life right in the very home we thought we were losing. Life will only be a disqualifying factor if you allow yourself to be defeated before you give yourself a chance to fight and push forward. Your ability to trust God over your circumstances is leaning on power you didn't know you had access to.

**People**—People will always be at the center of attention when it comes to the many setbacks you face. How, you ask? It's in our human nature to get ahead of those in front of us, which is why life will forever be compared to a race. And because of that, people will fail you, let you down, kick you to the curb, reject you, pass you by, and look over you for someone else—all for their own gain. They do not consider the repercussions they will cause in your life. People have a tendency to assess you based on their own expectations and standards for you. They are so quick to write you off before they give you a fair chance to prove yourself.

This typically comes from those individuals of major influence and importance to our life, such as a mother, father, family member, teacher, advisor, pastor, supervisor, manager, or mentor. I battled with abandonment issues growing up due to my father exiting my life at such a young age. I was left to maneuver in unchartered territory, while my mother had to raise a young man and teach me the best way she knew how. I did not become aware of these issues until well into my adult years. I began searching for validation and approval from those authoritative and influential figures in my life. I sought them out to confirm me, affirm me, and give me the approval needed to move forward. My feelings of rejection and disqualification came when I placed too much of my trust in those individuals. But I was still left with a void because I was looking for something in someone and I could not get the response needed.

We tend to expect people to play certain roles in our lives they were never meant to play. We set ourselves up for disappointments. I've learned, even with parents, the expectation for them to be everything we need them to be is not realistic. Parents, regardless of how we see them, are not equipped to be **everything** we need them to be. My eyes became open when I accepted that my father and so many others I put on a pedestal couldn't be what I needed them to be.

Sometimes people are just not physically, mentally, and emotionally equipped to play the roles they have in our lives. Even though we want and need them to, they just can't. This leaves many of us growing up having questions that we did not know the answers to, such as Why me? Why not me? Am I good enough? What makes me less desirable than others? Why wasn't I a good fit? Why didn't I meet the qualifications? Yes, I had to seek answers to all of those questions. And years later, I still did not have an answer. However, I was determined to find one. This is what being disqualified looked like to me, and I'm sure it may look that way to others.

We feel disqualified by the actions of others because we let them have authority over our lives to feel validated, but then they don't give us the approval we need.

When my father and my mother forsake me, then the LORD will take me up. (Psalms 27:10)

The Bible emphasizes parents because we hold them in high esteem in just about every aspect of life. God gives us the assurance that when our parents forsake us, reject us, or exclude us, he will give us everything we need. If God will protect, provide, cover, and love us when even our parents forsake us, then what more will God do when those who aren't even as significant as our parents disappoint us. Rest assured that when God has priority in your life, the power you gave to others is relinquished. God will free you from people's disqualification and give all the qualifications you need.

**Inadequacies and Limitations**—John 5:7-9 states that when Jesus met the man by the pool, he was unable to move himself into the pool. He called out for help, but no one answered. The people walked past this man daily, and he looked to them for help. In this scripture, we can see that this man had become a victim of his own inadequacies and limitations. He allowed himself to be a casualty of his rejections and disqualifications. The New International Version calls this man "The Invalid." This puts a claim on his condition because this man had become so consumed by his handicap that his actual name wasn't significant enough to mention.

## Disqualified—What Do You Mean?

Because so many of us have a specific handicap, disability, or limitation, we count ourselves out and delay our own progress. We **mentally** disqualify ourselves from potential success. We highlight our limitations so much that, just like the Bible called the man at the pool "The Invalid," people are calling and have categorized you by your limitations and inadequacies. This impotent man, "The Invalid," could not bring himself to roll or even crawl to get himself into that pool. But when **Jesus** showed up, he did not pick him up or help him up. Jesus didn't even call him by his handicap. Jesus simply said, "Rise, take up thy bed, and walk"! In other words, Jesus said, "**Get up** and **walk**."

Sometimes it's not your inadequacies and limitations that cause setbacks or that disqualify you, but it's **you**! British actress Emma Thompson said, "Being disabled should not mean being disqualified from having access to every aspect of life." We often believe and allow others to convince us that our limitations are our disabilities, our inadequacies are our handicap, and if we have a disability, then we don't qualify for a high quality of life. Everybody needs someone to speak into their life to give them a push, encouragement, motivation, and strength. You need someone to stir up your faith so you can believe that you can do just what you need to do to get where you need to be. The only person who has the power to totally disqualify you is **you**! Your inability to move forward and press past the various obstacles will cause you to disqualify yourself from all potential possibilities. John 16:33 says, "I have told you these things, so that in me you may have peace. In this world you will have trouble…." God promised in this life, you **will** have trouble, tribulations, setbacks, rejections, denial, loss, and ineligibilities, but he also said you **may** have peace. Setbacks are guaranteed, but your bounce back is conditional. You have a choice to wallow in your mess or fight with everything you have to get up! I mentioned earlier that all of these are inevitable.

Whether **life**, **people**, or your own **inadequacies and limitations** cause setbacks, rejections, and disqualifications, you can try your hardest to get it around them, but they will happen. The question is how will you respond? How will you overcome and recover from a major setback, a hard denial, a hurtful rejection, or an unfortunate disqualification? Here is your answer: **you get up**! And after you get up, remember **God** qualified you even when **you** and **everyone else** attempted to exclude you. Jesus said it like this, "Behold, I give unto you power to tread on serpents and scorpions, and over all the power of the enemy: and nothing shall by any means hurt you" (Luke 10:19). When everything around you is trying to destroy you and set you back, you have to know that God has given you the **qualifications** in **his** power to outwit those who are trying to invalidate you!

## Reflection

## Reflection

## chapter 2

# MAN VS. GOD'S CRITERIA

For as long as I can remember, I've talked myself out of so many opportunities and endeavors—convincing myself I did not qualify to do what was being asked of me. I knew what I could do, and I knew what I was called and even ordained to do! But I also had a list as tall as the Washington Monument of why I thought I wasn't good enough and why I didn't feel my skill sets were the perfect fit. I felt my influence wasn't great enough to make the impact on the world that I wanted. I wondered why I couldn't fit in or was never invited to be a part of certain circles, cliques, and meetings that I wanted to be a part of.

It's one thing when you know your own worth, skills, or expertise. When you are placed in a situation when you have to put **your** worth, skills, and expertise up against someone who, in your opinion, outweighs everything you have going on, you start seeing yourself as less than inadequate. But how can **you** and **I** have so much **greatness** inside of us yet allow our assumptions of others to affect us?

One of the hardest lessons I had to learn and accept is that man and God had two completely different qualification criteria. Shocked? So was I. It wasn't that I didn't know, but I spent many years wanting to give people the benefit of the doubt—where we were capable of seeing each other as

God sees us. But why would I ever think that the two could be even remotely close? If you ever spent a good amount of time in Sunday School, then you've probably heard that man is supposed to be the physical representation of Christ. But it quickly became evident to me that one was materialistic driven (man) and the other was simply out of a Father's love for his child (God).

The criteria of man's qualification often looks something like this: how much you have in your saving and checking accounts or whether you had a high credit score. Whether you possess a certain type of degree and where you earned your degree. It's where you're employed and what position or title you hold. It looks like whether you can finesse and hype up an audience and how well you sing, preach, or dance. How much you contribute to your local organization. Man's qualifications are always temporary, conditional, unstable, and forever changing, whereas God's qualifications are unconditional, unmerited, and have **no** prequalifying conditions.

Regarding man's criteria versus God's criteria about how you qualify in life, there will always be conflicting views, in both the natural realm and the spiritual realm. How we see ourselves and how others see us is very contrary to how God sees us. Isaiah 55:8 says, "'For my thoughts are not your thoughts, neither are your ways my ways,' declares the Lord." God was politely stating that we're not equal in our actions, thoughts, or anything else. God is saying, "I am the standard and your goal is to strive to be like me."

Let's give ourselves the benefit of accepting that man's ways will never match up to **God's** ways. Man's ways will always paint a fictitious picture of what something and who someone is, based on what we can see, hear, smell, and touch. But **God** will paint a picture based on how he **created** us, in **his** image. A perfect mixture of what **was, is,** and **what's to come!** God does not need a model to look at to paint the perfect picture of you. What God paints sets the standard of what should be modeled and how we should look and act.

Okay, let's go a little deeper into this illustration. A painter uses a palette, and the palette is used to arrange the various colors needed to paint their picture. The various colors on the palette represent what the painter needs and wants to paint the perfect picture. Not every color gets selected to be on the palette, and not every color gets used in the painting to create this so-called masterpiece. Some colors have been intentionally ignored, neglected, left out, and omitted from the painting. For whatever reason, the painter did not see fit to need, want, or use those colors. That painter has a set of qualities and qualifications where those colors that were omitted did not fit into the painter's plan.

In life, many of us on the surface may not be selected to be part of others' plans. That may include not qualifying for a job you want, or maybe the bank didn't approve you for the loan you needed. You may have even been terminated from a job or passed up on a promotion because you didn't meet the standards or criteria. Man's criteria are a perfect example of the painter. But what if we saw God as our ultimate painter? How would God use us, although man overlooked us, neglected us, and threw us out to the dirt?

Can I bounce back? Can I recover? Am I still valuable? What is my worth when I currently feel like I am no longer needed?

And the LORD God formed man of the dust of the ground and breathed into his nostrils the breath of life, and man became a living soul. (Genesis 2:7)

Oh, the confidence in knowing that God is an expert in using what man saw as the least and making it the greatest. When you don't meet man's qualifications, God goes out his way to pick you to be a part of his team. He validates you and affirms you to let you know that you're not only worthy, but you're worth it. God sent me directly to you by way of this book to remind you that you no longer have to fall victim to man's qualifications, but God is building you up and equipping you for better.

The Lord will open the heavens, the storehouse of his bounty, to send rain on your land in season and to bless all the work of your hands. You will lend to many nations but will borrow from none. The Lord will make you the head, not the tail. If you pay attention to the commands of the Lord your God that I give you this day and carefully follow them, you will always be at the top, never at the bottom. Do not turn aside from any of the commands I give you today, to the right or to the left, following other gods and serving them. (Deuteronomy 28:12-14)

A perfect biblical example of man's criteria versus God's criteria can be found in the life of Moses, in the book of Exodus. Moses was a leader who, through many trials and tribulations, led the Israelites out of Egypt, under the harsh leadership of the Egyptian king Pharaoh. But even though Moses was a great leader, he, too, faced much criticism, backlash, and setbacks. He dealt with the insecurities of wondering if he was a leader according to man's qualifications or if he was a great leader because God said so.

## Man vs. God's Criteria

The people who Moses led, set free from Egypt, and rescued across the Red Sea did not see Moses as a leader. Several times in the Bible, we see the Israelites complaining and blaming Moses for their suffering in the wilderness. Often, this is the picture of what it looks like through the eyes of man's qualifications. You try your hardest, make so many sacrifices, and put your life on the line, but people will still say you don't fit their standards. But if you keep reading, you will see that while man continued to doubt, count out, and exclude Moses, God at the same time is affirming and confirming Moses of who he is and whose he is.

In Exodus 3:10, the Lord commanded Moses to go to Pharaoh and demand he let the Israelites go. Moses, being fearful and doubtful, was unsure of his own ability to do what the Lord commanded. Moses confronted God and asked, "Who am I that I should go to Pharaoh and bring the Israelites out of Egypt?" This one statement brings back so many memories. I recall saying something similar on several occasions because I did not feel like I deserved to walk in what God was commanding me to do. The statement "Who Am I" hinders our own progress because we can't see who God has called us to be. Our desire to walk in man's approvals overshadows what God has called us to do.

While Moses struggles with this commandment and his insecurities, the Lord's response is not to speak to Pharaoh, but for Moses to speak to the Israelites. More often than not, your biggest critics, doubters, and naysayers are never strangers but those closest to you. Before Moses even got to Pharaoh, we had to deal with the Israelites. They questioned whether Moses was equipped to go before Pharaoh and who would go with him. But the Lord told Moses in verse 14, "Tell the Israelites, that I AM has sent me to you." Over and over, God will confirm that his voice and his Word will always outweigh man's voice, and even our own. And if our communication and communion with the Lord are infrequent, then we can only expect that when the Lord is speaking to us, our reception will not pick it up. And we wonder why man's voice will always remain louder than the Lord's.

Another example of how we talk ourselves into believing man's qualifications over God's is letting our own inner voices sit us down from a promotion where God is trying to elevate us. In Jeremiah 1:4-5, we see the Lord speaking to Jeremiah:

Now the word of the Lord came to me, saying, "Before I formed you in the womb I knew you, and before you were born I consecrated you, I appointed you a prophet to the nations."

God was promoting Jeremiah, but Jeremiah was talking himself out of being qualified for what God was setting him up to do. God had to remind Jeremiah that "before your own voice became your own hindrance, I created you to be the voice of the people." He said, "Before you allowed man's criteria to be the blueprint of your life, I had already equipped you with the true blueprint to follow." The problem is we long for man's qualifications to equal and equate to God's qualifications, and that will never happen. Our own voices often become the self-inflicted handicap that keeps us bound. This often stems from traditionalism, where we feel like we can't accomplish anything because of our age, status, and resources, or the lack thereof. We compare ourselves to our friends and families, seeking them for validation. Stop allowing man to set you up, set you back, and sit you down from positions and places where God has already established your foundation.

The year 2019 was a turning point for me when I walked out of that office, after being let go from a position I had held for about ten years—doing what I love to do and what I knew I was called to do. The decision wasn't because I had done something wrong but, rather, my time and season had expired. I left feeling empty, lost, stuck, and confused, questioning why did it happen and why now? Yes, I was in my feelings and very much upset. However, deep down inside, I knew this moment would come, and it had to happen. I knew God was pruning and refining me of habits, familiar places, comfort zones, and mindsets that were holding me down. How many of you know that as much as we WANT God's will to be done in our lives, it's not always easiest to accept?

After I was through processing what I was feeling and stepped back to examine what God was doing, I got the revelation that helped me get through. That year I decided not to live in the shadows or under the thumb of man's qualifications. Yes, I would respect and reverence it accordingly, and even submit when necessary, but I would not let it be the final word in my life. Naturally, it was a major struggle to unlearn because it was all I knew. It was a recipe I followed. I would not and could not move forward unless I had the validation from someone else.

I found myself holding man's qualifications over what I knew I heard God say concerning me. I allowed those people of influence whom I loved, respected, honored, trusted, and had given authority to speak into my life to hinder my steps and forward progression. None of these individuals did any harm or hindered me directly, but the harm and the hindrance came when I put them on a pedestal and their voices became louder in my ear, bigger than the voice of God! Their voices became the "Simon Says." Their voices became the "One, Two, Three, Red Light" that made me jump when they spoke. Yet when I heard the voice of God say move, go, jump, sit, speak, I became paralyzed because it wasn't what man told me to do.

So shall my word be that goes forth out of my mouth: it shall not return unto me void, but it shall accomplish that which I please, and it shall prosper in the thing whereto I sent it. (Isaiah 55:11)

In the history of mankind, there has never been a time when God spoke a word and it did not come to pass. You can read the entire first chapter of Genesis and see God speaking things into life. Rest in the assurance of knowing that God's Word has been dispatched to you concerning everything you're being equipped and prepared for. Once you allow yourself to be anchored in Christ and lead by his words, you will no longer feel the burden or the obligation of being a slave to inconsistency, temporal words, and standards that have been set by man. "All the promises of God are Yes and Amen" (1 Corinthians 1:20).

I don't know if you can relate to this, but let me speak something into your life. Do not become a puppet to man's qualifications. Allow yourself the freedom to see that while you may never match up to man's criteria, God sees you as a perfect fit for him. Let me pray for you:

Father, I pray right now in the name of Jesus that you help us tune our reception so that when you speak, we hear your voice louder than our own voices and the voice of man. Allow us to see ourselves the way you see us, and when we feel like we don't fit in or meet the criteria of man, you will be the only validation we need. Thank you, God, for your undying love and consistent assurance that keeps us covered and protected. In Jesus' name. Amen.

## Reflection

## Reflection

## chapter 3

# Your Worst Chapter

*You can't judge an album by a single song, it's like judging a book by only reading a single chapter.*

*—Trevor Rabin*

Have you ever sat back, looked at your life after a major disaster or delay, and said to yourself, "I **hate it here**"? No? Okay, well maybe I'm the only one. Imagine tuning into a much-talked-about movie or a critically acclaimed TV series. You're watching season after season and episode after episode. You're laughing, you're crying and on the edge of your seat, anticipating how it will end. You reach the end of the movie or season finale, and you're sitting there in pure disappointment, thinking to yourself, *Is this it? Is this how it will end*? You feel like you've wasted weeks, days, and hours of your life for a horrible ending—time that you can never get back and no way of knowing what's to come.

That's how life can feel. You get to a place where you hit rock bottom and ask yourself, "Is this it? Is this how it will end?" I recall a season in my life when I had gotten several rejections back to back, within an eight-month timeframe—from being terminated from a position I loved, to being picked over for several other positions I sought after, and then getting a few "not approved" for some opportunities I wanted. Each of these rejections, setbacks, and not-approved moments really weighed heavy on me. I began to question my own skill set, confidence, and ability to excel in current and future opportunities. I started thinking, if I can't even hold a position that I thought I was pretty good at or land a new position that I desire, and if I am getting picked over for opportunities that I **know** I qualify for, then something, must be wrong with **me**. (I'll go into more details about that in a later chapter).

Yet having experienced so many setbacks in a row, I just knew it would be a long road ahead, going straight toward a dead-end. However, these weren't my first rodeos, dealing with rejections, setbacks, and denials. I've experienced my fair share of this my entire life, and it is never easy to digest. It never feels good when you're in the midst of it all. You feel a new kind of pain and weariness. Every situation felt like the worst, like someone was purposely ripping a band-aid off an open wound!

For instance, my family's favorite game is UNO.® My family loves this game, and I love it even more because I currently hold the record for the most wins! I often feel like I have an advantage because I know how to play the game, I understand the game, and I know how to play the hand I'm dealt. But every now and then, after several victories, I find that the hand I'm dealt does not always work out in my favor. I get dealt a questionable hand, or after a few rounds in, when it looks like the hand I was dealt will be another victory for me, my opponent comes along and throws out a number of "Draw-2s" and "Draw-4s," a few "Skips" and a couple of "Reverses." UNO is yelled and just like that, they're out and I lost. I saw my winning streak vanish and found myself questioning whether I was, in fact, as good as I thought I was in this family favorite game.

What am I saying? Life will catch you off guard, just like a game of UNO. Some days your life will seem like it's going great, without a care or worry in the world, when suddenly, opposition will hit and you will find yourself being "Skipped" or picked over for someone better. Or what happens when everything is going your way and you get thrown a "Reverse" card, and now a life that was once going your way is going the complete opposite direction? All your good days have turned into bad and trying days. And to make matters worse, on top of being Skipped and having the tables turned on you with Reverses, you now have to deal with Draw-2s and Draw-4s. Those situations add extra stress, causing major obstacles, weighted burdens, and unnecessary hurdles. It gives you more to handle than you feel you can. And when it's all said and done, you're now sitting at the table playing this game of life, watching everyone scream "UNO and OUT." They are excelling, succeeding, progressing, and advancing, and you're left with a hand full of cards. You have more than you started with and you're losing!

I remember asking God on more than one occasion, "Why am I losing so much in life if I'm playing the hand I was dealt?" In my mind, I was doing just what I was supposed to do. I wasn't trying to peek into anyone else's hand, I wasn't trying to cheat to win, and I was genuinely playing the hand I was dealt. I asked God that question and the room got completely silent. The Lord answered my question with a question: "The hand you were dealt, does it represent a day or a lifetime?" He went on to explain, "If the hand you were dealt represents a lifetime, then you've killed any chance of trying again. But if the hand you were dealt represents a day, even if you lose, you live to play and try again!"

It took me a few days to process what the Lord shared with me. Then I was led to Psalm 37:23, which says, "The steps of a good man are ordered by the LORD: and he delighteth in his way." Regardless of the hand we're dealt and the life we have, God leaves us with the assurance that our steps are uniquely orchestrated by God to work out for our good. Romans 8:28 says, "All things work together for the good of them that Love the Lord...." Allow me to speak this into your life, "**The fight is fixed!**" Although it may look like you're losing and your life is going every way except the way you wanted it to go, God wants you to take a glimpse into the future to see that you win in the end! No matter the cards you hold in your hands and no matter the cards your opponent holds, I need for you to know that there isn't a Skip, a Reverse, a Draw-2, or Draw-4 that can mess up the steps or the path God has you on. You must play the hand you're dealt and trust the God that created the hand you were dealt.

I struggled with seeing God in the many situations I was in. I had a hard time accepting that God was orchestrating some of the worst chapters in my life. It seemed as if my life was filled with more "Worst Chapters" than better chapters. More hard days than good days. More questionable days, than certain days. But thanks be to God, they weren't my final chapter! The moments of life's rejections will most certainly feel like the final chapter of your life. In the back of your mind, you can hear a voice whisper, "It's over." You see the end credits rolling, and even as you're getting ready to walk out of the theater, you think it's over! You already sense there is no bouncing back, no do-overs, no retakes, and no recovery. And in your mind, the sound of the life support machine has already started flatlining, without any hope of resuscitation. I know you're probably asking yourself, "Is it really that serious?" Or maybe you haven't experienced a major loss, setback, or failure?

These feelings that I speak of, and that some of you may have experienced, are real feelings. They should be acknowledged, addressed, and given the attention they deserve to properly heal from them. But do these feelings often translate to feelings of defeat, failure, incompleteness, and lack of confidence and self-worth? It takes a certain amount of confidence to go after something.

The Bible says, "Faith without works is dead," so if I am going after something or in pursuit of something, then my actions are prompted by faith. Therefore, if I am moving in faith, I am trusting God to meet me where I'm going. For whatever reason, I don't get there, not because I can't make it but because I have allowed someone or something to prohibit me from getting there. My faith and my trust in what God has promised me are now being questioned. And now, not only do I have to deal with the stench and residue of defeat and failure, now my trust and faith in God are in conflict.

I am reminded of what John 16:33 says: "In this life you **might** have peace, but you are guaranteed to have tribulations..." Every chapter in your life will have a place for hardships, a place for your disappointments, a place for all matters you wish you could avoid. However, just like in a book, in order to reach the end with a full understanding of what you read and how it all comes together, you must read each and every chapter. So when you find yourself face-to-face with one, two, or three of your worst chapters in life, you must understand that it's not your final chapter. Your worst chapter is simply a few pages—it's the climax of the book to add some shock value, strengthening and turning points for the finale!

While dealing with my rejections, displacements, setbacks, disqualifications, and disapprovals, I had to acknowledge that what was happening was really happening. I could not pretend that I wasn't mad; I could not pretend that I wasn't hurt. I had to acknowledge and accept all my feelings and deal with them accordingly. The worst thing we can do when faced with any trying situation is ignore our feelings. Thomas Jefferson said, "Honesty is the first chapter in the book of wisdom." Regardless of what chapter you're on in life, be honest about how you feel about the direction your life is going in. One of the many life-changing lessons I learned came from my godbrother, Joey: "It is ok to **not** be ok." He went on to say that "you have to give yourself that space and time to properly deal with what you're dealing with." And I did that. I recognized my anger, hurt, and similar feelings. I began to process them and dealt with them accordingly.

The anger, bitterness, resentment, weariness, lost and confused feeling you get when you suffer a major setback, disqualification, loss, or displacement is like a plant. "**What you feed will grow**." And you can choose to feed the seeds, or you can let it die. May I suggest that you process the feelings, but don't live in the moment or dwell in the situation? It happened—accept it, make some changes and adjustments, and press forward. Do **not** allow temporary setbacks to cause permanent damages in your life. After processing my feelings, I could see that while this felt like my worst chapter, it was not! Yet it was an indication that greater days were ahead!

One of me and my wife's favorite TV shows to watch together is NBC's *This Is Us*. This show is such a perfectly written and directed emotional roller coaster. It follows the lives of Jack and Rebecca Pearson and their three kids, Kevin, Kate, and Randall. After the death of the rock of the family, Jack Pearson, Rebecca's husband and the kids' father, the show follows the family on a long, winding, up and down road to healing, recovering, adapting, surviving, and maintaining a family of their own. The show jumps around from the present time, to the past, and occasionally, a sneak preview to the future to show where many issues stem from that are affecting them throughout their lives.

The show gives you so much to take in and process, episode after episode. The family always has some major, heart-wrenching, mental and emotional obstacle to face that always seems to stem from the death of their father. All three kids and their mom have to go on with life and grow up through their teen and adult years facing major setbacks, losses, and trials. And while my wife and I are watching, we're on the edge of our seats waiting and anticipating to see just how the Pearson family will recover and bounce back from it all.

Every episode paints the picture that there's no way the Pearson family can come back from this—from the loss of their father, complication in a pregnancy, alcoholism, severe anxiety, unexpected deaths, to the birth of a child with special needs and deep-rooted family issues. While the show continues to take us through loops and obstacle courses, it always gives us hope for better days in future episodes. The writers always find a way to give the audience a sense of relief by showing us that in the midst of all that they've gone through, the characters find peace and healing by reflecting on their relationship with their father.

Thinking about the many episodes of *This Is Us*, I began reflecting on my own life and how many episodes I have had—filled with chaos, hurt, pain, fear, anxiety, and setbacks. Some episodes left me with so many uncertainties about how it would end and whether one episode was worse and if another would be the last episode. But just like in the show, while our father isn't Jack Pearson, we can find peace and healing and relief in our heavenly father. Whatever stage of life we're in, we can look to God for all answers! God is the writer, the producer, and the director. He has total control of the things we feel we're losing control over. The episodes and chapters in your life you feel you may not make it through, God will give you a "To Be Continued" while he works on your life behind the scenes.

So this season may feel like the **worst** chapter, and you may want to give up, quit, and not pursue anything. But I am here to tell you that your worst chapter is not your **final** chapter. Keep pressing, keep going, keep reading on. Your rough chapters are preparing you for your greater chapters. Every chapter you live, overcome, and conquer is a step closer to another chapter better than the previous. Jeremiah 29:11 says, "For I know the thoughts that I think toward you, saith the Lord, thoughts of peace, and not of evil, to give you an *expected end.*" God has an expected end for your life and an expected chapter for your book. God has an expectation that will not end with your worst chapter. You remain in this chapter because you chose to stay there.

When I was going through, I immediately decided I did not want to stay there—feeling bitter, mad, angry, and upset.

I was very intentional in moving forward and pressing on. I did not want to allow my defeat to hinder my progress. The Apostle Paul said it like this, "Being confident of this very thing, that he which hath begun a good work in you will perform it until the day of Jesus Christ" (Philippians 1:6). You must understand that God is the author, creator, and finisher of your book. He is the father of your chapters. God started and finished your book way before you were born, and even as you live your life day to day, God is still working on the various pages of your life, adding plot twists, grand finales, and punchlines. God has you on his mind **constantly**, and he has the chapters of your life in his thoughts, hands, and plans. God is allowing you the grace to go through these trying chapters because for every bad chapter you encounter, God will show up and perform a greater work for your greater chapters!

You still have **years** of chapters to live, and you still have chapters to write, but I assure you that **this** chapter right here—the one that feels like the cruelest chapter—is actually the prelude for your **greater** chapters! This chapter is not your final chapter. Your greater is a page turn away!

*"Breathe. This is just a chapter.*
*It's not your whole story."*

*—S.C. Lourie*

## Reflection

## Reflection

## chapter 4

# It Had to Happen

*"Dread it, run from it—destiny arrives all the same."*
*—Thanos (Avengers Infinity War)*

*With overwhelming and exciting anticipation, it gives me great joy to say that I want to be disqualified today! I can't wait to get rejected! I really hope I get looked over and passed up for an opportunity. I can't wait to be told they selected another candidate.* ***Yes!*** *I live for moments like these….* says **no one ever**! Never has anyone spoken such words. However, you must know without a doubt that rejections, disqualifications, and being overlooked, passed up on, turned down, etc. will inevitably happen. And when they do happen, you must ask yourself, "How will I respond? How will I internalize those harsh, hurtful, and disappointing moments?" When these unfortunate circumstances happen, your response may not change the outcome, but it will certainly change your perspective.

So if you will, grant me the access to come into your space and help you. First things first, no one **wants** to go through anything. If we could have it our way, we would live the most easy-going, stress- and obstacle-free life forever.

## It Had to Happen

No one wants to be rejected, turned down, or ineligible. But everything you've gone through in the past and right now, and everything you've encountered and faced, **had to happen—it was necessary!** That situation that sent you to a place of grief, anger, failure, fear, and feeling unworthy was key to your breaking, but just like the songwriter said, "When it's God that does the breaking, he breaks you gracefully." So when I say, "**It had to happen** and **it was necessary,**" I am speaking to what you have not yet seen yet or witnessed. I am speaking to you from a position that already places you at the finish line. You're already overcoming. You're already being restored everything you lost. That's what I am speaking to right now, in the midst of what you're going through! Because **it had to happen!**

My setback was a part of a bigger plan than I could see or wrap my head around while it was happening. I had to realize that this life I live is not mine, but it is GOD's property. God can and will do whatever he needs to do, to us and with us, to fulfill the purpose in the life set before us. And if it takes sending us through one, two, or three moments or a series of unfortunate events, filled with setbacks and failures, with the purpose to birth an ultimate success story, then that's what God will do. He will bring the greatest stories and testimonies out of some of the worst moments in your life. Join me as I look at the life of two of my favorite characters in the Bible—Job and Joseph. Let's see what they went through and how they overcame the trials, struggles, and setbacks in their own lives. As you read about their lives, take a hard look at all that you're going through. May their stories encourage you that what you're going through now is just a comma in your sentence, and God is the period to complete it.

Come here **Job** (Job 1:1-20). It is written that you suffered and went through some **major**, life-changing, life-threatening, and life-altering trials that nearly took you out. Scripture says one day while you were home minding your business and living your life, you got word that all your kids died in a tragic accident, and from that moment on, it was one thing after another. All your servants were killed, you lost all your farm animals, and even the very house you lived in was destroyed? And to make matters worse, on top of all that, you had to endure painful pus-filled bumps that covered your entire body from head to toe? And yet you still lived to tell the story? But how? How was Job able to endure, bounce back, and overcome such tragedy and devastating setbacks? I believe if Job was still alive today, his response would be, "**It had to happen!**"

Let's look at **Joseph**. It's written in Genesis 37:1-36 that you also went through and overcame some harsh rejections, obstacles, and displacements. You were thrown into a thirty-foot-deep, empty well. You were left for dead. And not only were you thrown into an empty well and left for dead, but you were sold for twenty pieces of silver by your very own biological brothers. This was all because you told them about a dream you had. Please tell me, Joseph, just how were you able to recover from that to tell your story? How were you able to overcome being brutally displaced and excluded, especially by the people you love? I imagine Joseph's response was, "**It was necessary!**"

You see, both Job and Joseph, two completely different characters, with their own respective stories in the Bible, had to go through some trials that could and should have literally killed them. Their sanity was on the line, their mental and physical health was on the line, and their families were sacrificed and compromised. Everything they lived for was taken from them, and yet they survived to tell the story that **it had to happen** and **it was necessary**! But the story doesn't end here. While it had to happen and was necessary, understand your pain, rejections, disqualifications, setbacks, failures, etc. are connected to God's promise and His purpose. Your story doesn't stop at your setbacks.

After Joseph was thrown into an empty well, he was left for dead and sold by his brothers. Several chapters later in Genesis chapter 41, after a series of events, we learn that Joseph is no longer in the empty well. He is not dead and no longer sold into slavery and has been elevated to governor. **Joseph's pain was necessary**! Sometimes the gateway to our purpose and promise is buried in a pit of pain. Just like when you watch a movie, the magic that happens on screen is a result of all the chaos and madness that happens behind the scenes. Joseph may not have seen his seat as the king's right hand had he not seen the bottom of his pit.

The necessary pain that should have killed you was covered in God's grace. So not only did it spare you, but it blessed and positioned you. If what you're going through or have gone through was so necessary, that means God saw you and said you were the perfect candidate for the trials. You were built to handle the turbulence and equipped for pain because God knew that, of all people, **you** were the one who would overcome. The necessary pain you overcame was the same pain that took someone out.

Job's story starts in chapter one, and by the end of the second chapter, he literally loses everything! By the time you reach Job 42:10 (the very last chapter of the book of Job), you will see the Lord healing Job and restoring to him all that was taken from him. We see the Lord blessing Job with more than he had lost. As the popular cliché goes, Job got double for his trouble! **Job's pain had to happen!** Job's overflowing restoration came because of his willingness to endure. It was his choice to endure because he could have given up. But when the pain in your life is so great, you know the only way you will survive is by the grace and hand of God on your life. That alone gives you just a little bit of encouragement to endure.

Job's endurance was solely in his trust in God. He had no idea that he would be compensated for his pain. Job didn't expect to be blessed for his burden. But when the pressure and the pain **have** to happen, God does not let his children go through blood, sweat, and tears without rewarding them for their endurance, "to appoint unto them that mourn in Zion, to give unto them beauty for ashes, the oil of joy for mourning, the garment of praise for the spirit of heaviness..." (Isaiah 61:3). When the pain and setbacks have to happen, make sure your life is grounded and rooted in God's insurance. God will make claims on all the burdens and pain you suffer and endure. The payout is far greater than the trial. Romans 8:28 says, "And we know that all things work together for good to them that love God, to them who are the called according to his purpose."

For your own sanity and spiritual growth, you must know that your past and present setbacks were placed in your life to catapult you beyond where you are now or where you could have gotten on your own. Your destiny is built on the foundation of God-ordained, organized chaos. Your setbacks are strategically designed and tailor-made for you for your benefit, for now and for later! God knows just what's needed to position us for greatness, even when it doesn't seem good, even when our feelings get hurt, and even when life circumstances are the opposite of what we would like them to be. It's for a reason. When the Bible says, "**All things** work together for **his** good," your "**it had to happen...it was necessary**" situation was a great gift stuffed inside an unpleasant package—all for **your** good!

A lot of what we go through that we would probably have liked to avoid had to happen. The heartaches and pains that come with this journey are necessary and are all part of God's plan! But let's look at things from a different perspective. What if all that we go through—the setbacks, the trials, the pain, and the burdens—didn't have to happen? What if it wasn't necessary? What if I could or did avoid every painful experience, every major loss, or every hard setback? How do you think you personally or the life you live right now would be?

In an episode of *This Is Us,* the scene opens with one of the main characters, Randall Pearson, talking to his therapist, working out some issues he's struggling with in the present day due to some issues that occurred in his past. The scene shows him having severe anxiety attacks, wondering what his life would have been like had his father not died. What would have happened if he could have prevented his father's death? As the episode unfolds, it cuts to a flashback in a fictitious world. We find Randall in his teenage years at the scene when his father was supposed to die. But instead of his father dying, he survives.

The story goes on because his father has survived and is now living. As Randall and the other characters in the show go on with life, they realize that with their father now living, many of the opportunities they had in their real lives no longer exist. This included their childhood, their bond with one another, the colleges they chose, their careers, and the families they have. What had to happen, and what was necessary, did not happen!

While Randall is talking to the therapist, he realizes that first, there was absolutely no way he could have prevented his father's death. Second, had his father not died that night, Randall's life would have gone in a completely different direction, and he would not have met his current wife or have three beautiful daughters. He would not be a successful councilman, and his relationship with his mom would not be as great as it is in the present day.

As this chapter ends, consider what if Job had never lost all that he lost? What if Joseph had never been thrown into that pit and sold into slavery? What if Moses had never been placed in a basket and sent down a river? What if Jonah had never been swallowed by the fish? What if the woman with the issue of blood never had it? What if the woman at the well didn't live the life she was living? What if Paul and Silas had never been locked up? What if Jesus had never gone up on that cross?

It is natural for us not to want to go through those tragic moments. It's natural for us to try to avoid at all costs those moments of hell and high waters. But the way God's math works, we may never understand. Paul said in 2 Corinthians 12:7-9, "I was given a thorn in my flesh. I pleaded with the Lord three times to remove it." The Lord responded to Paul, "My grace is sufficient for thee: for my strength is made perfect in weakness..." God's power is made perfect in our painful moments. So without those painful experiences, we may never truly experience the mighty power of God.

## It Had to Happen

A major setback in my life was arriving at my mom's house one morning only to discover that she had suffered a massive stroke. It caught me completely off guard. My entire world was rocked to the core. I was helpless, scared, angry, and filled with a ton of emotions racing through my mind and my body. I questioned everything about life, God, my mom's life, and my own life just to find some answers about why it happened. I even asked God if he could turn back the hands of time so I could prevent it from happening. I was asking for everything I could to change the situation I was in. But nothing changed. Those "**it had to happen, it was necessary**" moments, may never make any real sense, and honestly, there is nothing anyone can say to help you process it all or give you any real peace regarding what you're going through.

I can't tell you how many countless nights I woke up, hoping and praying it was a dream. I needed answers and I needed them quickly. In that moment, the only place I could find answers was in the presence of the Lord. I had to spend some long hours praying, crying, listening, and battling back and forth with my own wants and needs. During that time of going back and forth from seeing my mom in the hospital to seeing her in a nursing home, I found **some** peace in knowing that what had happened to my mom had to happen so she could live to see another day. Many may not understand or even accept this, but the massive stroke she suffered that day had to happen to prevent her possible internal battle with taking her own life.

It is my prayer that you can see how you had to suffer a major loss to gain your abundance. You had to go through a nasty divorce to find your God-sent spouse. You had to get fired from that job to position you for your next, or to birth that successful business. You had to get denied for that house loan so God could position you for your dream home. You may have been shut completely down physically, emotionally, and mentally in order to save you from yourself.

Motivational Speaker Dr. Willie Jolley wrote a book in 1999, and his book title became a well-known catchphrase that everyone still quotes today: *A Setback Is a Setup for a Comeback*. The title speaks to how God ordains and orchestrates the trials for our life in the form of rejections and disqualifications, then creates a platform that will launch us toward our destiny and his promises. Everybody wants to bounce back from their setbacks and failures, but I believe God wants us to spring forward. God **wants** us to learn, grow, testify, and prosper from our pain! As I look back over my life, I now realize that everything I encountered, endured, was exposed to, and had to go through did not happen in vain. My pain came attached to a purpose, connected to a promise, and it launched to a place far better and greater than where I was. I say all the time that I could not have orchestrated such a plan for my life, filled with so much chaos, pain, heartbreak, failures, setbacks, and disqualifications, only to see how all of that could birth such a miraculous blessing in my life! **It had to happen...it was necessary!**

## Reflection

## Reflection

**chapter 5**

# Identifying With Your Setbacks

*"Tough times don't define you; they refine you."*
*—Carlos A. Rodriguez,*
*Designed for Inheritance: A Discovery of Sonship*

Think about and honestly attempt to answer the following question: ***If disqualification and rejection were a picture, what would it look like to you?*** I'll wait...

Now that you've had a few minutes to think about it, if you're having a hard time trying to paint a picture in your head of what **disqualification and rejection** looks like, then go ahead and Google the two words and see what pictures you'll find. You might be surprised to find that not one picture is of you. Not one single picture looks like you. No picture even comes close to resembling an image of you. Not one! Yet when faced with constant, trying situations, it is very easy to see yourself through the eyes of your adversity.

We create an illusion of ourselves in our minds that **we are our setbacks**! But I am here to tell you that very thought is incorrect. It's a lie, it's a trick, and its purpose is to sabotage your reality. You are not who your setbacks say you are. Your setbacks are not a part of your DNA, and they are not a part of your makeup. But they **are** a part of the plans for your life (For I reckon, that the **suffering** of this **present time**… Rom. 8:18). Therefore, you must expect that it will happen. Your life is a big puzzle, and those setbacks are intricate pieces needed to complete your puzzle.

Because I have experienced several denials and many stumbling blocks, I can only imagine how you feel, what you're going through, and the thoughts you may be thinking. I know how I felt, and I know what I was thinking when I was going through. I mentioned in a previous chapter that with all the rejections, setbacks, exclusions, and denials I endured, I honestly thought something was wrong with me! I felt ashamed, embarrassed, and too prideful to even speak to anyone about it. I felt like I was the only one dealing with it.

I took my setbacks personally, internalized them, and made them a part of me! I allowed what I was going through to turn my run into a jog, and from a jog back to a walk, until I found myself not even walking or moving. I was standing there lost, with no energy, confidence, or motivation to move forward. I allowed my setbacks and disqualifications to paralyze me! These were real feelings that I was facing, but they most certainly were not God's will for my life. And it's not his will for yours either! Yes, you will go through; everybody will experience a wilderness. However, you don't have to make your wilderness experience your permanent living arrangement. Your wilderness is supposed to teach and grow you, not destroy and kill you.

Yet I was standing there overcome with shame, embarrassment, anger, lack of confidence, and low self-esteem.

I found myself standing there clothed in my setbacks, wearing my disqualifications, suited in rejections and disapprovals. And failures had me spiritually, mentally, and almost physically paralyzed, feeling all alone—all because I let my trials defeat me, I let my setbacks overcome me, and I let myself become consumed with everything coming against me. It was **that** moment when I quickly reminded myself that what may feel like my **worst** chapter was not my final chapter!

Suddenly, I heard the Lord whisper in my ear, "Danny, you are fearfully and wonderfully made" (Psalm 139:14). "Danny, I will make you the lender and not the borrower; you are the head and not the tail, and you will be above and not beneath" (Deuteronomy 28:12-13). As I heard this affirmation from the Lord, I knew what was happening—the Lord was rebuking who I thought I was by affirming me of who he created me to be. Let me explain. Christ specifically says I am the "Lender" and not the "Borrower," the "Head" and not the "Tail." The choice of words used to speak to my identity painted a clear picture of where I needed to be, and who I was created to be.

Christ does not desire for his children to live in the deficit nor to make a home in the wilderness. While we may have to experience the deficit and while we must pass through the wilderness, living in such conditions should not be our standard. Being the "Borrower" and being the "Tail" means you are or have experienced setbacks that have caused you to now be behind and in need. But God said we are the **lender** and the **head**, and we're to live **above**! God called his children to be ahead and able to provide! He said I need for you to be above, so you can bring others up. But such is life, and most setbacks, rejections, and disqualifications will leave you conflicted and literally feeling unable to live ahead, to be the lender and to live above.

The subway system where I live has a popular slogan, "If You See Something, Say Something." This slogan is used to protect its riders, by encouraging them to speak up if they see anything suspicious, strange, or out of the ordinary that could possibly put others in danger. The slogan challenges others to be bold and confident to share what they suspect or see. This illustration came to me because so many times when we're going through or dealing with the residue of the trials we face, we find ourselves taking on the name of what we've gone through. If I'm used to failing at something, I will begin to identify myself as a failure. If I am constantly getting rejected, I may identify myself as a reject. If losing has been the common card in the many hands I've been dealt, then it's natural for me to see myself as a loser. But I hope you know that you are not what you've been through or going through. That is not your identity.

When you see yourself in a strange, suspicious, and out-of-the-ordinary situation causing delays and heartaches, you need to say something. You need to speak to it and cast it down so it does not attach itself to you. You have the authority and the power to speak up and speak against that which is contrary to God's will for your life. Mark 11:23 says, "Truly, I say to you, whoever **says** to this mountain, 'Be taken up and thrown into the sea,' and does not doubt in his heart, but believes that what he says will come to pass, it will be done for him."

When you speak to your situation, you must believe what you're speaking. Before you can see yourself delivered, you must first speak it, then believe it. Recognize the power that has been given to you and walk in it. Luke 10:19

declares, "Behold, I have given you authority to tread on serpents and scorpions, and over all the power of the enemy, and nothing shall hurt you." Stop downplaying the authority that has been given to you to speak to any and everything that may come up against you. Your power rests in your belief. If you believe you are what your setbacks say you are, then that's how you will live. But if you believe your setbacks don't determine your place, position, or outcome, then you won't identify yourself as such.

But I get it. I understand. When you've been set back so many times, it's hard to see yourself another way—outside of the struggle, the trials, the hell that has marked your life. It is especially hard to see yourself the way the Lord sees you. Even with perfect vision, it still needs to be renewed! My vision needed renewing. At one point in my own life, I honestly thought my last name was Danny **Failure**, Danny **Loser**, and Danny **Rejection**, along with so many other names that speak to being held back, never seeming to be able to move forward. But setbacks can be devastating, and when you've experienced so many back to back, you begin to see your failures, setbacks, and rejections as the norm. You begin to identify yourself as your setbacks. Even after God has told you exactly who you are, you still struggle to see yourself the way God sees you!

I preached a sermon once titled "I **Am** Who **God** Says I **Am**," which was about Moses receiving his charge to confront Pharaoh to free the Israelites. But before Moses can grasp the courage to go before Pharaoh, he has to confront his inner man and who he perceives himself to be versus how God sees him in this very moment. The sermon places you in the shoes of Moses, having to confront how **we** see ourselves versus how **God** sees us.

I used the illustration of three mirrors: Mirror 1 was broken and shattered. Mirror 2 was dirty and stained. And Mirror 3 was perfectly clean and polished. Each mirror stood as a representation of how we see ourselves. The broken mirror represents all the setbacks in your life, all the heartaches and pain, the abuse, the rejections, the heartbreaks, the sickness, and illnesses, all the bad news and unwanted reports. The dirty mirror represents the sin in your life—the dirty, filthy, tarnishing sin that so easily besets us, everything you do and have ever done. Both mirrors are symbolic of how we see ourselves in the mess that we've gone through and the mess that we're in—the broken, abused, rejected, tainted, stained, failed attempts, shattered dreams, and all of life's mishaps.

I placed these two mirrors in the face of my audience and had them take a hard look at themselves. Interestingly, I noticed they did not have a problem looking at themselves in the dirty and broken mirrors. They seemed comfortable looking at themselves and seemed to easily relate to the conditions of the broken and dirty mirrors. Yet when I placed the perfectly clean mirror in their face, the feeling of unease quickly fell upon them. They began to look away, cover up their faces, and close their eyes. The reservation and hesitation to look at themselves in the perfectly clean mirror was obvious. It seemed it was easier for them to see themselves in the broken and dirty mirror instead of seeing the whole person as God created them to be in the perfectly clean mirror.

Yes, our righteousness is nothing but filthy rags, but by the grace of God, we don't have to look like what we've been through. After I finished preaching, I did some reflecting of my own and the revelation hit me. This is how I saw myself. This is how I viewed who I was, even after God told me who I was! I allowed myself the unhealthy space to wallow in my setbacks instead of seeing myself being set up for greatness! Others could even see and acknowledge my greatness, but I couldn't see it for myself.

As you continue to journey through this book, I encourage you to peel back the layers that your setbacks have caused, where you can still be broken, turned down, and still see yourself as Christ sees you through that perfectly clean mirror. Stop calling yourself a failure and call yourself favored. Stop calling yourself a reject and start calling yourself redeemed. Stop answering to what the world wants you to be and what the world is calling you and start telling the world who God has called you to be.

For years, we have had to deal with the world telling us who we are and are not. Now it's time we remind the world of who we are. Because once Christ calls you by your name, you no longer identify with the trials you face or the mess you're in. Saul, known as the Chief of Sinners, had a reputation for murdering Christians, met Jesus on the road to Damascus, and got his name changed to the Apostle Paul. Jacob, known for tricking his brother Esau out of his birthright, had an encounter with God and got his name changed to Israel. When God changes your name, he changes your lifestyle. The Bible says, "Old things have passed away, behold, all things become new." Christ no longer sees you for who you were, but he sees you for who he created you to be. Our struggles do not validate us, they simply prove that God is bigger than we will ever be. When we lean on him and see ourselves the way he sees us, we will never need to be validated by the world ever again.

When a baby is born, parents receive a birth certificate that has all the information to tell who that baby is, where the baby was born, and other vital information that confirms the baby's identity. When that baby becomes an adult, some of the same vital information is transferred on a state-issued identification card or a driver's license. These documentations serve as a primary form of identity. It is law that the information on your state-issued identification card matches the individual holding it. You should always have your state-issued identification card on you at all times. It is often used to prove your identity to authority figures or when making purchases. Without this card, you could very well be mistaken for someone else. Without this card, you would have a hard time trying to prove to someone just who you are. Without this card, your identity would become questionable, and it would be hard for people to identify you. And if you happen to lose your driver's license, birth certificate, or state-issued identification card, the only way to obtain a new one is to go back to the office that issued them.

What am I saying? Before parents received their child's birth certificate, God gave us our identity. He had already appointed us and ordained us with the calling on our lives. He created us with a purpose and for a purpose. Our identity is often mistaken when we forget who we are and whose we are. Our identity is lost when we stop believing who God has called us to be and start believing who the world wants us and is telling us to be. We lose our identity because we become disconnected from the person who gave us our identity. Now is a good time to pause, go back to the Father, and ask him to renew your identity. Ask God to remind you of who you are.

Pope John Paul II said, "We are not the sum of our weaknesses and failures; we are the sum of the Father's love for us and our real capacity to become the image of His

Son Jesus." I particularly like this quote because it further confirms our identity in Christ, that we are not the result of our setbacks and disqualifications. But we are the result of the love of our Creator. God sent his Son, Jesus, to die on the cross for the sins of the world. We don't have to die in the identity of our setbacks but live in the glory of who God has called us to be. You are not the rejections, the setbacks, and the disqualifications you've encountered. You are not the who or what your obstacles say you are!

I know your mother or father may have left you, family turned their backs on you, teachers all through school said you wouldn't be anything, and you've struggled to find your place in the corporate world. Every time you try to take five steps forward, you get knocked ten steps back. But Christ left us with some reassurance in His Word that confirms that our setbacks now will be our victory later. Jeremiah 29:11 says, "For I know the thoughts that I think toward you, saith the Lord, thoughts of peace, and not of evil, to give you an expected end." God has plans for your life, and your identity reflects his promises. Your life and all the things you go through are just a part of a bigger plan God has for you!

Now that you've been reminded that you are not your setbacks, here is the piece of the puzzle that starts the process of bringing it all together. Before I could fully see myself the way Christ sees me and understand that my identity was not in my failed attempts and trials, I had to give myself permission to walk in my freedom! I walked in the promises that God has ordained over my life. His Word says, "Delight yourself in the Lord, and He will give you the desires of your heart" (Psalm 37:4). Christ is our true deliverance from all setbacks and sins. He gives us the power and authority to free and release ourselves from the bondage of our setbacks. Christ delivered me from all of my past, present, and future setbacks. While I am already delivered, I still must go through the process. But I can rest assured that while I am going through the process, God is with me the entire way.

# Reflection

## Reflection

## chapter 6

# Trust the Process

Webster's Dictionary says that the word "process" is a series of actions or steps taken in order to achieve a particular end. I would like to add my two cents to the definition: *It is the dash (–) in between the year you're born and the year you die (ex. 1980–????).* From the time I entered this world, my entire life has been made up of a series of processes—a process to grow, a process to learn, a process to trust God, a process to act on what I believe, and a process to live out my God-given purpose on this earth before I die. I did not adjust to the various processes as well as others or as well as I thought I should. Yet I quickly learned and have come to accept that there are two guaranteed dates in this world: the day you're born and the day you die. What happens during the process in between those dates is solely up to you.

The process must happen, and you have to go through, endure, and overcome to complete it. You have no idea what that process looks like, what it involves, what the risk factors are, and what you will gain and lose along the way. All you know is the day you're born, the day the process starts, and how you maneuver through the process will determine how it ends. That's what makes that "dash" (–) in between your birth year and death year such a mystery because you're blindly trusting God while going through life's process hoping for a successful end. Your process in life is to trust God to guide you and lead you through, beginning the moment you opened your eyes to start your day. You wake up, say your morning prayer, grab your coffee and your bag, and you head out the door, in full stride, awaiting the next steps that make up your **process**!

In this chapter, I want us to focus on three parts. I pray it will give you clarity and insight on how to trust the process. I want to talk about *1. Trusting the Process, 2. Following the Instructions, and 3. Passing the Test.* You must go through the process. Trust the steps taken and follow the instructions provided. When steps one and two are done correctly, you pass the test.

## Trusting the Process

Now that we're on the same page with what a process is, let's dig a little deeper into what trusting the process actually looks like. Let's discuss the uncertainty, the unknowing, and the not-so-sure series of events that make up your ordained steps, which will eventually lead you to your purpose. I mentioned that with any process in life, you really have no idea what will take place during those steps. As you may think, many variables and factors come into play to create the right process for the right outcome for you. However, despite our own logical thinking, neither the process nor the outcome has anything to do with the factors or variables but, ultimately, the God-ordained plans for your life.

The trusting part in the process is a one-word answer: "**faith.**" However, the longer definition means accepting the steps you have to take to get to your destination, knowing and believing that you're being led and guided by Christ Jesus, regardless of what it may look like. Your process may come with several good days, good news, good moments, and great outcomes. And then you might find yourself on the opposite side of the playing field where your process may come with a series of bad days, ugly steps, tragic moments, and sick and tired of being "sick and tired" outcomes along the way. But allow me to put a pin right here and focus on those unfortunate steps. These steps in the process may come in the form of rejections, ineligibilities, hard trials, and major failures.

The steps of a good man are ordered by the Lord, and he delights in his way. (Psalms 37:23)

"**The process**" involves the hard, strenuous, intentional steps you have to actually take and go through to get to the place you desire to be. Just thinking about it gives me anxiety. I know I am not the only one who can relate to this. I dread having to go through what I perceive to be unnecessary. But in reality, **it is necessary!** If there is a desired place to want to be, a desired result you're trying to achieve, or an accomplishment you want to obtain, then you must go through the process. There is no way to avoid it or get around it. And it hurts. But why does it hurt? The process hurts because you're putting your mind, body, and soul through intentional steps while completing several tasks and overcoming various obstacles. You encounter many attacks and defeats because you're trying to reach the place you desire. Your **desire** to reach your destination is the reason you must not only go through the process but also trust the process. If I did not **desire** to achieve greatness, if I did not **desire** to grow, if I did not

**desire** to overcome and conquer, then I would not need to go through the process!

Every morning, I commute to work from the suburbs of Maryland to downtown Washington, DC. My commute involves riding the subway. Unless I drive my vehicle, the only way for me to get to work is by train. So my journey begins. I board the train at my starting location and find my seat (or I stand depending on how crowded the train is). As the doors close, I brace myself for a long ride into the city. When the train leaves the station, it enters a very long, dark tunnel. For those who suffer from being claustrophobic, this could be a real problem. There are twelve stops from the time I board the train until I have to get off to go to work. My entire commute takes place underground, going in and out of dark, dirty, creepy, long tunnels, without any visual of what's ahead of me or what's behind me. Often the train could get stuck in the tunnel. Other times, the train would malfunction and I'd have to off-load the train in the middle of my commute and wait, not knowing if and when the next train would come. This caused some major delays in reaching my destination. I had to literally put my trust and faith in the train conductor to safely get me through the dark tunnels and to my destination!

Every morning, my desired destination is to get from my house to my job. And every evening my desired destination is to get from my job back home to my family. And the only way to get there is to trust the driver of the train to get me through those dark, dirty, creepy, long tunnels, without any visual of what's ahead or behind me. There was no way around it, no way over it, and no way under it, and I couldn't go backward. If I wanted to get to my destination, **I had to go through it.**

Trusting the process is just what it sounds like. You're trusting the steps, the commute, the delays, the transfers, the **entire** process it takes to get to your desired destination. You don't know what's coming your way. You don't know what delays you may encounter. You don't know what setbacks you have to endure. You don't know what obstacles you may have to jump over. All you know is that you **must** get there by any means necessary, regardless of what comes your way. And you're going to trust **God**, who is the head conductor, to lead and guide you through it all.

## Following the Instructions

1. Teacher gives student clear instructions.
2. Student follows the instructions.
3. Student successfully completes the task because he or she followed the instructions.

When trusting the process, you must be able to follow the directions and instructions given. For example: I am trying to get from point A to point B, so I put my destination's address into the GPS. However, If I totally ignore the directions given and decide to go my own way, I cannot be upset if I get lost or don't arrive at my destination on time. God did not give us **his** word for us to completely deviate from it and follow our own questionable instructions.

> The fear of the LORD is the beginning of knowledge, fools despise wisdom and instruction.
> (Proverbs 1:7)

It is impossible to trust the process if you're still trying to handle the process on your own. Now, let me go ahead and put this out there—I have **always** struggled with following instructions. I struggled as a child, I struggled as a student, I struggle as an adult, I struggle as a husband, and I struggle as a father. This is definitely an area where I constantly ask the Lord to help me. But I've learned over the years following instructions is so hard for so many, including myself, because we have to put our trust and faith in something or someone else other than our own ability.

If I am following instructions to get to a place that I desire to be, I have to first relinquish control and follow someone else's steps.

> Trust in the LORD with all thine heart, and lean not unto thine own understanding. In all thy ways acknowledge him, and he shall direct thy paths. (Proverbs 3:5-6)

If we're going to trust God to lead us and guide us through the many steps and processes on this journey, it is essential to follow the instructions given. Or else we subject ourselves to failures and destructions. Many setbacks, rejections, and delays happen in our life when we decide to do things our own way. We skip steps along the way and in the process of following the instructions given. No student has ever succeeded by ignoring their teacher.

Allow me to paint a picture to give you a better understanding of my point. My wife and I went to a Sip and Paint for a date night. I have never done one before, so it was new to me. Before we arrived, my wife had already assumed that this would be fairly easy for me because I am kind of the artistic one out of the two of us. So she just knew my painting would come out better than hers. We arrived and were shown to our seats. In front of us, we had a blank canvas, four paintbrushes of different sizes, and a palette with several different colors of paint. At the front of the class was a canvas with an already painted picture on it. The instructor began by explaining the supplies in front of us, how to use them, and what we would be painting.

In my mind, after staring at the already completed painting, before the first set of instructions were given, I was already a few steps ahead. As the teacher gave the first few steps on what to paint and how to paint, I followed along and instantly realized that this was a lot harder than I perceived. Again, as I said earlier, before the first instructions were given, I had already decided what I wanted to do. Too many times, when instructions are given, we're often already trying to figure out an answer to a problem before we're given the complete instructions. This causes us to miss information or misinterpret the instructions, and we find ourselves, having made several mistakes or lost.

As I struggled through my painting, I looked over at my wife's painting and noticed she was following the teacher's instructions. Her painting looked much better than mine. I got discouraged because I realized that my picture did not match the teacher's picture, and my picture didn't look as pretty as my wife's. This was all because I did not follow the teacher's instructions to achieve the desired outcome. You see because I did not follow the instructions as they were given, I had to suffer through some delays, setbacks, corrections, mistakes, cover-ups, and do-overs—trying to fix what I messed up.

Such is life. Many of the obstacles we face are mainly due to our lack of obedience in following directions. We want to get somewhere or achieve something so bad and, in a hurry, we ignore the steps to properly and safely get there. And we find ourselves full of discouragement and frustration simply because we failed to heed the instructions and directions we receive in life.

> For the protection of wisdom is like the protection of money, and the advantage of knowledge is that wisdom preserves the life of him who has it. (Ecclesiastes 7:12)

Following directions will not only get you to where you need and want to be, but it will also save your life from **unnecessary** pain, headaches, setbacks, and delays. When you follow the instructions, you can plan accordingly for various roadblocks and detours. You can't avoid them all, but you can plan for them when they arrive.

## Passing the Test

In every stage of life, you will be required to take and pass a test before you can move on to the next stage. Whether you're in elementary school, middle school, high school, college, the workforce, or the military, you must pass a test to move on. But let's be honest, who **really** wants to go through the test-taking process with the uncertainty of even passing? I know personally, growing up, I was **never** a great test taker. I could do great work, amazing projects, and write incredible papers and essays, but I was a horrible test taker. But regardless of how bad I was at taking tests, I still had to take the test and still had to either pass or fail the test. Nonetheless, the results of the tests I've taken throughout my life were determined by how well I studied and if I was prepared.

Life's tests will come in various forms. Some tests will come in the shape of trials, losses, setbacks, temptations, rejections, disapprovals, obstacles, or unplanned life circumstances. But unlike school and the workforce, when you're given a study guide to help you prepare for the test, you have to learn how to prepare for the unexpected. You have to expect that around every corner, you just might have to deal with a test that may leave you questioning whether you will pass or fail. But I want to provide some assurance that even if you don't have a study guide or a map to guide you, you have everything you need to pass the test. That's right, you have been equipped with everything necessary to pass a test you had no idea was coming and no way to plan or prepare for. Why? Because your test is **tailor-made!** (I'll let you digest that for a minute).

As a preacher, I have worn my fair share of suits and learned the difference between a "store-bought" suit and a "tailored-made" suit is that a store-bought suit is not guaranteed to fit you. When you purchase it, there is a big chance you'll be unable to wear the suit right out of the store. But a tailor-made suit is custom-made to fit every curve, muscle, length, and width of your body. A tailor-made suit is made to fit you and only you. The beauty of knowing that your test is tailor-made is that any and everything that comes your way has been cut, stitched, hemmed, sown, measured, and pieced together to fit you in a way that's only suited to your needs and lifestyle. Everybody's test is tailored for them. Your test may appear similar to others, but the results and answers to the test will be different. This means someone else didn't make it through the one obstacle you were able to overcome, jump over, and get through. When you didn't think you would pass the test that nearly took your life, God placed his hands on you and became your study guide to lead you through.

**God will test you according to what he knows you can handle.** I am reminded of Moses in Exodus 14:21, when he was presented with a test he didn't think he could pass. Moses had just freed the Israelites from Egypt. And just when they thought they were clear and free, Pharaoh and his soldiers were now on the hunt for Moses to kill him. Moses and the Israelites found themselves stuck between a rock and a hard place. After fleeing from Egypt, Moses now had a large body of water, the Red Sea, in front of him, and Pharaoh's armies closely approaching behind him. In the natural realm, Moses and the Israelites could either jump into the Red Sea and drown or surrender to Pharaoh and be killed.

This is how life's test will come at you. Just when you think you've overcome one obstacle, another one presents itself without any warning. Moses was not prepared for this test. He knew he had to outrun Pharaoh and his army, but he did not think he would have to deal with both Pharaoh and the Red Sea. What could Moses do now? Here is a good place to let you know that **if God chose you for the test, he already knows the outcome**. Romans 8:18 says, "For I reckon that the suffering of this present time is not worthy to be compared to the glory which shall be revealed." So when you're smack dab in the middle of a test and you find yourself being suffocated with anxiety, fear, worry, and doubt, and you have no idea how you will make it through, know that God always has a tailor-made plan in place for you.

When Moses and the Israelites were standing near the Red Sea with Pharaoh behind them, God commanded Moses to lift up his rod and raise his hand. At that moment, the miraculous happened. When Moses followed the instruction God had given him, to lift his hands and raise his rod, the Red Sea separated, allowing Moses and the Israelites a straight, dry path to walk through to get to safety. And the same Red Sea intended to destroy Moses and the Israelites ended up destroying Pharaoh and his army. When your test is tailor-made, it has already been ordained for you to pass. Your struggles, your doubt, your fears, your worries, and your uncertainties have all been factored into your test so the spiritual algorithm will line up for you to get the victory! **God has his hand in every test you encounter for an expected outcome.**

Trusting the process is not easy, but it's possible. And the reward is greater than any delays or rejections you will ever face. When you look at what you've gone through, or will go through, you can have confidence in knowing that your process has a God-ordained exit strategy in place to help you get through and grow through, to become a better you.

> But he said to me, "My grace is sufficient for you, for my power is made perfect in weakness." Therefore, I will boast all the more gladly about my weaknesses, so that Christ's power may rest on me. (2 Corinthians 12:9)

## Reflection

## Reflection

## chapter 7

# It's the Who that Matters to Me

In 2018, I was working at my "good" government job that I had for over seven years, from a government contractor all the way to a federal government position. Suddenly, I hit a dead end and a glass ceiling. My family's financial responsibilities were exceeding my biweekly paycheck. I needed a new job **bad**! So I jumped out there to start seeking new employment. I searched and searched, going on website after website, applying to everything—only to get rejection after rejection. I got a few calls for a couple of telephone interviews and a few in-person interviews. Every time, I got the response, "I'm sorry Mr. Prince, we decided to go with another candidate for this position."

As always, you find yourself questioning everything about yourself and your life. Was my resume not impressive enough? Was it because I didn't have a certain degree? Did I not have the skill set they were looking for? Maybe they just didn't want or like me! Come on, I can't be the only person who has wrestled with these thoughts? After months of stressing, feeling unhappy, undervalued, and unappreciated at my current job, all while being shut down from countless employment opportunities, the Lord led me to speak to a family friend. I know that sounds cliché, but who am I to argue with God? I met with her and told her I was in the process of looking for another job. She told me there was no guarantee, but that she may be able to help. She provided me with clear instructions on what to do. She told me to send her my resume, go to the job's website, complete the application online, and wait for further instructions. Sounds good, but then, I became discouraged. I had been down this road on several occasions, and in my mind, I knew how this would end.

However, I got out of myself and decided to trust the process, follow the instruction I was given, and pray that I pass the test (refer to Ch. 5). Months had gone by, and I hadn't heard anything. I just knew this story would play out the same as it had in the past. After months of waiting, I began emailing and throwing subliminal messages to this family friend, checking to see if she got my email and if she could use it or submit it on my behalf. One day I got a call asking if I could come in for an interview. The interview started just as other interviews. The only difference was that each of the interview panelists said the lady who received my resume spoke very highly of me. They said based on her recommendation, they were excited to even be interviewing me. To make a long story short, a few weeks after that interview, I left feeling good, yet somewhat uncertain, and still holding on to past emotions of failure. I checked my email to find that I was selected for the position, and I was hired a few months later.

I share this story with you because often, our past and previous rejections and letdowns are grounded in the What, Where, When, Why, and How. And we find ourselves feeling hopeless for any future accomplishments. This was a clear example of how I didn't feel qualified for the position, but my qualification was in the family friend who took my resume, believed in me, placed my resume in the right person's hands, and spoke highly of my name. While in this story I referenced this friend as being my qualification, this is exactly what God does for us when we feel we aren't qualified, equipped, or fit for something based on our lack of confidence. Christ assures us through his love, grace, and mercy that in him, we **are** qualified, equipped, and suited for the very things man said we don't or wouldn't qualify for.

At times in our lives, our abilities will more often than not match our desires. Our ability to do something may disqualify us from something we desire. You want that new job that pays more, yet you don't have the skill set to apply or qualify for it. You want to write that book, but you don't feel you're capable of writing it. You want to buy a house, but your finances and your credit score disqualify you from even applying. You want to start your own business, but you don't have the money or the resources to start it. Have I come down your street yet? Okay, let me say it this way: your desires to accomplish certain things in life can be so big, yet you don't possess, or may feel like you don't possess, the physical or tangible abilities to achieve them. And in those moments, we must fully rely on what God has spoken over us and who God has called us to be.

But why is it so hard for us to believe and accept that **God's** qualifications will always trump man's qualifications for our lives? Is it because we can't see past what man can do and has done for us and believe that God can do and has done way more than man? Who's more reliable and dependable—man or God? Do we really believe when the

Bible says, "Now unto him that is able to do exceedingly abundantly above all that we ask or think, according to the power that worketh in us" (Ephesians 3:20)?

Let's break this scripture down for some practical application to help us on this journey. The first part says, "**now unto him.**" You must be able to identify when reading this that Christ is **him** and not **you**. Be not mistaken—these three words remove you from the driver's seat and places you in the passenger seat, where you belong. It's comfortable for us to always want to be in control until we realize we don't have much control over anything. The scripture goes on to say, "Now unto him... **that is able to do** .... When you and everyone else has counted you out, deemed you unqualified, unfit, and unequipped for the task, remind yourself of this declaration: when **you're not** able, **God is** able! Here is my favorite part of this scripture: It says, "Now unto him ... that is able to do **exceedingly abundantly above all that we ask or think....**" Not only is God **able** to do what is needed to validate us, confirm us, qualify us, and then some, he will go over and beyond just being **able.** He will exceed our expectations, requests, prayers, petitions, and our thinking to do **more** than we ask of him.

This scripture speaks of what God can do and will do not just because we asked, but simply because of his **love** for us and because **he is.** We put our trust, our hope, and everything else in **him**! The scripture ends with "now unto him... that is able to do exceedingly abundantly above all that we ask or think... **according to the power that worketh in us.**" Whose power is working in us? It is Christ's power! The only power man can possess is the power connected to the source. When we plug our inabilities up to Christ's abilities, we gain full access to qualify for the things we should have been disqualified for. We must be confident enough in the true power source, which is Christ, to disconnect from the temporal power source of man. Understand that once we allow Christ to be our qualifying factor, we're giving unlimited access to a well that never runs dry! You can drink the Christ and never thirst again.

Let's look at the book of Jeremiah. We see a young man battling with his own insecurities because he feels inadequate to accept the calling being placed on his life. He doesn't feel qualified. He doesn't feel he is equipped for the assignment. He doesn't have the degrees or the certifications. He doesn't have the years or the experience. Jeremiah says to the Lord, "I cannot speak for I am a child" (1:6). How many of us have parted our lips to make excuses and speak against what we know the Lord is calling us to do, or what we have a desire to do, because we don't feel worthy enough for the assignment? But I love this part. The Lord immediately steps in (sometimes you need the Lord to step in, interrupt you, and cut you off in mid-sentence). He says to Jeremiah, "Stop saying you're a child because wherever I send you, I will go with you. And whatever I command, you will speak" (1:7). The Lord goes on to tell Jeremiah, "Do not be afraid of their faces because I am with you and will deliver you, in my name" (1:8).

This entire conversation between the Lord and Jeremiah rings in my head often because I find myself in Jeremiah's shoes, quoting similar excuses, such as "I am a child." But my excuses **now** are a little different. They sound a little something like, "I don't make enough money," "I don't have the credentials," "I can't speak like so and so," "I don't have degree letters behind my name," "I don't know enough Bible to speak on this." But I am encouraged because, as I read,

I see how the conversation started with Jeremiah and the Lord. It didn't end the way Jeremiah thought it would. You see, Jeremiah thought when he told the Lord that he wasn't qualified for the assignment because he was a child, the Lord would let him off the hook to wallow in his excuses and limitations. But instead, in Jeremiah's moment of weakness and feeling incomplete, God said to him: **I am your qualification!** When I created you, I qualified you. "I formed you…I knew you…, I consecrated you…, I appointed you…" (1:5). Everything the Lord spoke to Jeremiah regarding who he was calling Jeremiah to be, and what he was calling Jeremiah to do, he said you will do it **in my name**! God's name was his qualification! God's name was his total access. God's name was the key to unlocking every door Jeremiah needed. The door to his confidence, the door to his self-esteem, the door to his breakthrough and his calling was rooted in the doors that God opened.

What if I told you that you were overqualified for everything you desired simply because Christ has qualified you? You have to become what Christ says you are. When the world says you aren't fit for an assignment, a task, a job, a calling, a shift, and a movement, you must be able to reach into your arsenal and pull out the help you need to defeat your insecurities and your doubters. 1 Peter 2:9 says, "But **you** (every person reading this book) are a chosen generation, a royal priesthood, an holy nation, a peculiar people, that **you** should shew forth the praises of him who hath called you out of darkness into his marvelous light."

Stop allowing your untamed inner voice to be the defeat that takes you out and sits you down. People will never see you for who you are until you look in the mirror and you see **who** God has created you to be. Who is the "**who**" in your life that sets the tone for your success, your identity, and your life! Ask yourself that question, identify those individuals, and do yourself the favor of sitting them down and allowing Christ to sit high on the throne! He is your qualification.

I remember spending some quiet time and writing in my journal one day, and I began to write what I heard the Lord say to me. He said, "Danny, you're putting too much weight and expectations on people. That is why you keep getting a '**no**' from the people you want, long for, and desire to hear a '**yes**' from. In this season, your '**yes**' will come from the unexpected, and it will carry more weight in your life than the expected."

I heard a preacher once say, "None of us are Worthy, but God looked at us and saw us as Worth it." He looked at each one of us and saw us as worth qualifying. Christ put his name as a reference on the application he cosigned for you to be approved. He stepped in to be the judge, the juror, and the lawyer for a case we were supposed to lose! He didn't have to, but he did! You see, the big takeaway for you in this chapter is this: your qualification is not in the What, Where, When, Why, or How. But it's in the **who**! When the **what** you're doing isn't enough, when **where** you're going becomes blurry, when you struggle with **when** something will happen, when you don't know **why** things are happening the way they are, and when you can't even begin to figure out **how** it will work out, rest assured that when Christ is your **who**, you can't fail. You will win every time.

Often, instead of God fixing the issues that broke, he fixes the person who's broken. It's God that gives you the boost, the endurance, and the confidence to do what's needed to bring you up to a qualifying level. Remember you were already qualified—you just needed the push and the faith to see yourself the way God sees you. Philippians 1:6 says, "Being confident of this very thing, that ***HE*** which hath begun a good work in you will perform it until the day of Jesus Christ." Christ is your qualification, and you must be confident in Christ and the "Good Work" he started in you to know that you're qualified not by your own abilities, but by **his** power. Take this confidence and apply this to every area of your life. Whether you're a receptionist or a GS-15, **you're qualified!** Whether you're married or a Widow, **you're qualified!** Whether you hold a GED or a PhD, **you're qualified!** Whether you're a stay-at-home mom or dad, or a lawyer, **you're qualified!** Whether you have to adopt children or have your children biologically, **you're qualified!** Whether you're a cashier or the CEO, **you're qualified!** Whether your credit score is 500 or 850, **you're qualified!** Don't allow your current situation to stop you from trusting God to pursue your next situation. When you remove *you* from the equation and put God in the equation, you have a problem that's already been solved.

## Reflection

# Reflection

# #WORDSFROMAPRINCE

So you've reached the end of this book, but your journey continues! What's your next move? I have shared many of my toughest moments and trying stories to show you that you are not alone. And you will never be alone. It is my hope that if you should ever feel like you're all by yourself in your storm, in your moments, in your situations and obstacles, that you will turn to the pages of this book. I pray they will give you the confidence to face every situation that tried to count you out, set you back, and disqualify you. I pray you will return to the pages of this book for affirmation and confirmation. May the obstacles I had to overcome be a testimony to you. If God did it for me, he will certainly do it again for you. Don't count God out when things get tough and you feel like you're by yourself. Don't count God's Word out when you find yourself lost for your own words. Don't count yourself out when you find yourself sitting in the eye of multiple storms crashing down on your life, all at one time. Know that God does **all** things well, and some of his best work is shown during some of our worst moments.

I know the path you're on may seem long and daunting, but I assure you, you're a lot closer to the finish line than you think. But it is my prayer that you don't just arrive at the finish line but arrive whole, healed, and ready to keep going even after you've made it. Every step you take is a step closer to your breakthrough, your healing, and your deliverance. Everything you've gone through is a page in **your** chapter that creates stories in **your** book, which is still being written. Things may not be what you would like them to be now, but in due season, you will gain, you will heal, you will grow, you will flourish, and you will excel if you do not give up.

It is my prayer that the information shared, the stories told, and the illustrations painted in the pages of this book will give you the encouragement and assurance needed to go after everything your heart desires. So much life awaits you outside of your fear of being validated, confirmed, and accepted. Your obstacles were the key to the doors that needed to be open for you. God did not make a mistake when he made you and me. He didn't make a mistake when he allowed those trials to happen to us. It had to happen. Less we do not forget, we are God's perfectly created and well-put-together children. God poured his everything into us when he created us. But I know how hard it is to see and believe just how perfect we are in his sight when it feels like we're constantly being defeated daily. And with all the hell you've gone through and will go through, it's even harder to believe that your life is ordained and uniquely orchestrated to include all the ups and downs and for you to have an expected end. Your life is a masterpiece puzzle, and God is the winning piece. With him, you cannot and will not fail. With him, you can have certainty that your best is yet to come!

I declare and decree, in the name of Jesus, that all I had to go through was necessary and it had to happen. God, I thank you because I went through and I came out stronger. I know in this next chapter, you will begin to hear, see, speak, and walk in your season of: **You're hired! You've passed!**

**You're approved! You're qualified! You've been accepted! You will advance to the next grade! You've been selected for the position! Your skill set matches the qualifications we're looking for! We're choosing you as our candidate! And your services are appreciated and still needed!** When God Qualifies the Disqualified.

#WordsFromAPrince

# About the Author

Pastor Danny Prince II embodies what it means to be a mentor, encourager, and leader.

Born and raised in Washington, D.C., Pastor Danny accepted Jesus Christ as his savior at the age of sixteen while attending St. Stephen Baptist Church located in Temple Hills, Maryland. He accepted his call to preach and teach the gospel of Jesus Christ under the leadership of Senior Pastor, Bishop Lanier C. Twyman, Sr. He became a licensed minister in 2008 and an ordained elder in 2013.

Pastor Danny served in ministry at St. Stephen for twenty-two years. Though he has had various leadership roles within the local church, Pastor Danny's heart has always been with the youth. With over fifteen years of experience working in youth ministries, he has worked with every stage of youthhood, ranging from toddlers to adolescents and young adults. Danny has been afforded to share the Gospel on several platforms, both locally and nationally, he is often called on to speak at retreats, camps and conferences.

Pastor Danny is passionate about what God has called him to do, and it is evidence in his worship and his serving. Many of his closest friends and colleagues describe him as "fun, creative, and high-energy." His creative approach to preaching and teaching allows him to understand and engage with youth on many levels.

Pastor Danny currently serves as the Teen Pastor at the Abundant Life Chapel in Largo, Maryland, where he serves under the lead Pastor Tayo Tychus.

Along with Danny being a preacher, teacher and youth and teen advocate; he's an author. Danny wrote and released his first book titled *"It Had to Happen"* in April 2021. His book is intended to encourage and help his readers understand how to accept and overcome life's setbacks, disappointments and losses through Christ. Danny's book can be purchased on his website and Amazon.

He is married to his best friend Angela Prince, and together they have three beautiful, energetic, and anointed daughters: Aaryn, Avery, and Allyson.

His motto is *"I am a Servant of Christ before I am a Minister of the Gospel; I am a Follower of Jesus before I am a Leader to His people... I am NOTHING without CHRIST!"*

www.ingramcontent.com/pod-product-compliance
Lightning Source LLC
LaVergne TN
LVHW010106110826
845155LV00028B/507